BLUEBONNET at the MARSHALL TRAIN DEPOT

By Mary Brooke Casad

BLUEBONNET
at the
MARSHALL
TRAIN DEPOT

Illustrated by Benjamin Vincent

ETBU →

WILEY COLLEGE

PELICAN PUBLISHING COMPANY
Gretna 1999

To my Texas and Pacific family with Marshall roots: my parents, Ben and Nancy Kelley Oliphint; my uncle, John Pegues Kelley, Jr. (a native of Marshall); my grandparents, John and Mary Kelly Kelley; my great-grandparents Ely Thomas and Avie Kelly; and my great-grandparents Walter and Exa Kelley

The author gratefully acknowledges the following for their contributions: The Board of Directors of Marshall Depot, Inc., Audrey Kariel, Marjorie Perkins, and Tony and Laurie Overhultz.

Library of Congress Cataloging-in-Publication Data

Casad, Mary Brooke.
    Bluebonnet at the Marshall Train Depot / Mary Brooke Casad ; illustrated by Benjamin Vincent.
        p. c.m.
    Summary: Bluebonnet the armadillo visits the newly renovated train depot in Marshall, Texas, and learns a little about the history of the railroads.
    ISBN 1-56554-311-4 (hc. : alk. paper)
    [1. Armadillos Fiction. 2. Railroads—Trains Fiction.
3. Marshall (Tex.) Fiction.]   I. Vincent, Benjamin, ill.
II. Title.
PZ7.C265Bn 1999
[E]—dc21
                                                                    99-20920
                                                                    CIP

∞ ©

Printed in Korea

Published by Pelican Publishing Company, Inc.
1000 Burmaster Street, Gretna, Louisiana 70053

BLUEBONNET at the MARSHALL TRAIN DEPOT

The Marshall town square was still and quiet as Bluebonnet the armadillo roamed around the old courthouse. Although it was night, the courthouse shone brightly, lit by hundreds of twinkling lights.

"How beautiful," Bluebonnet said. "I've heard this 'Wonderland of Lights' festival is the largest of its kind."

She ambled around slowly, looking at the lights.

"Marshall has lots of festivals," she said to herself. "I'd like to visit the Fire Ant Festival. Those fire ants sure do make a hot, spicy meal for us armadillos!"

Bluebonnet turned at the corner and began walking down Washington Street.

"But for this visit, I've come to see the Marshall Train Depot," she said.

The sun was coming up when the little traveling Texas armadillo arrived at the Marshall Train Depot. The depot was a large, red brick building that stood between two railroad tracks. Bluebonnet peered through the fence and wondered aloud, "How do I get to the depot?"

"This way!" She heard a voice behind her, and felt something furry brush by her tail. She turned around in time to see a cat running to a small, red building. Bluebonnet cautiously moved toward the building. The cat swished his tail back and forth, waiting for her patiently.

"So, you'd like to see the depot?" He closed his eyes slowly, then opened them wide.

"Yes," said Bluebonnet, shyly.

"Well, I'm the one who can show you around. The name's T. P.," he said, twitching his whiskers.

"I'm Bluebonnet," she said. "Tell me, what does T. P. stand for?"

"Texas & Pacific," he said proudly. "I'm named for the railroad that made Marshall famous."

"To get to the depot, we'll have to walk through this underground tunnel," T. P. said, and motioned for her to follow him down the steps.

"Wow!" exclaimed Bluebonnet. "It's like a big armadillo burrow!"

"This tunnel was built in 1940 to make a safe passage to the depot below the tracks," said T. P. His voice echoed against the walls.

"But the Texas & Pacific railroad began long before that . . . and in an unusual way," he said. "In 1858 the track had been laid between Caddo Lake and Marshall. Rail service was due to begin, but the locomotive, which was being shipped by riverboat, had not arrived. So three yoke of oxen were hitched in front of two boxcars and one flat car. The oxen pulled the cars from Caddo Lake to Marshall. That was the first rail transportation used by this railroad company."

They walked out of the tunnel into the light.

"And here's the depot!" said Bluebonnet. "When was it built?"

"In 1912," said T. P. "Lots of cats have worked here, ridding the depot of mice. It's my job now." He scratched his head. "So, why have you come to Marshall?" he asked.

"I travel all around Texas," said Bluebonnet. "I want to learn about the history of the depot and the railroads. It looks like you're the one who can help me."

T. P. playfully pawed at the bow on Bluebonnet's sunbonnet. He rolled over on his back and batted Bluebonnet on her nose.

"Hey!" said Bluebonnet, stepping back.

T. P. laughed. "I've never had an armadillo friend before," he said. "But I'm glad you've come to visit."

Bluebonnet smiled. "Thank you," she said.

"C'mon in, Bluebonnet," said T. P., heading for the door. "Let me show you around."

"Here's where the passengers purchase their train tickets," said T. P. "People have been riding the trains from Marshall for over a hundred years."

Bluebonnet smiled at T. P. "I'm glad you're here to tell me all about it," she said.

TEXAS & PACIFIC
RAILROAD

CHICAGO

MARSHALL

T. P. pointed to a map. "For several years, the trains from Marshall only ran to Longview, Texas and Shreveport, Louisiana. Then, in 1871, Congress granted the company a charter to build a railroad from Marshall all the way to the Pacific Coast. That's when the company was named the Texas & Pacific Railway Company."

They climbed the stairs to the museum.

"Wow!" said Bluebonnet, pointing to the pictures. "Look at those steam locomotives."

"It took lots of coal to feed the fires that made the steam engines go," said T. P. "Those were the engines used to pull the passenger and freight trains. Before the days of cars and airplanes, people traveled by train."

Bluebonnet and T. P. watched model trains speed along tiny tracks.

"Marshall was the T & P general headquarters. People came to Marshall from all over the world to work for the Texas & Pacific railroad," said T. P. "Entire families worked for the T & P."

"It must have been like a great big family," said Bluebonnet.

"Yes," said T. P. "Everyone in Marshall knew the train schedules and listened for the train whistle."

Outside on the balcony, Bluebonnet and T. P. could see all around town. T. P. pointed down the tracks.

"In 1873, Marshall became home to the railroad shops, which were built up and down these tracks," said T. P., waving his paw. "The shops built the equipment needed to run the T & P."

The two walked around to the other side.

"That's the Ginocchio Hotel," said T. P., pointing to a building near the depot. "Railroad passengers used to say they served the finest meal between New Orleans and Denver."

Bluebonnet gazed over the balcony ledge. For a few moments she imagined Marshall in the early 1900s . . . a busy, bustling railroad town.

T. P. seemed to be daydreaming about the past, too. He yawned and stretched sleepily, warming himself in the sun.

"So, the days of the Texas & Pacific railroad are no more," said Bluebonnet. "What happened?"

"After World War II, the railroads declined," said T. P. "T & P retired its steam locomotives and used diesel engines. In 1976, Texas & Pacific Railway Company merged with another railway company, Missouri & Pacific. Years later, the company became the Union Pacific."

"But the trains still run through Marshall, even today," said Bluebonnet.

"There are not as many as there used to be, but the freight and passenger trains still come through Marshall," said T. P., nodding his head.

Quietly, they crept down the stairs and followed the porch around the depot.

"This depot building has a special story, too," T. P. said. "Years ago, it was almost torn down."

"Who saved it?" asked Bluebonnet.

"The people of Marshall," said T. P. "Especially the children. The children wrote letters and drew pictures of the depot. They asked that the depot be restored. And they saved their pennies to help with the cost."

"So the people of Marshall helped restore the depot so we can all learn about the railroads," said Bluebonnet. "It certainly does make a swell museum."

UNION PACIFIC

"Come on out to the caboose, Bluebonnet," T. P. said, running across the depot yard.

"The caboose?" Bluebonnet asked, out of breath as she ran after him.

"That's what the last car of a train is called," said T. P. "But you don't see many cabooses anymore."

"That's what I like about Marshall," said Bluebonnet. "There are lots of historical things to see."

T. P. jumped up on the caboose, and Bluebonnet climbed aboard after him.

"So, this is what it would be like to ride a train," said Bluebonnet. "I've had lots of travels, but never on a train. Of course, you know all about trains and have probably ridden many times."

T. P. hung his head. "No," he mewed sadly. "I've never ridden a train."

Whoooo! Whooooooo!

Bluebonnet jumped straight up into the air! "What's that?" she gasped.

"Why, it's an old steam locomotive!" exclaimed T. P. "I've never even seen one like that, much less ridden one."

From their perch on the caboose, T. P. and Bluebonnet watched the train pull up beside the depot and stop.

Suddenly, Bluebonnet turned to T. P. "Let's go!" she said. "Let's go for our first train ride together."

"But I can't," hissed T. P.

"Sure you can," said Bluebonnet. "Let's just run and jump on. We've always wanted to take a train ride. Trains go away, and trains come back. You won't be gone long."

"Bluebonnet, I do believe your traveling ways have rubbed off on me," said T. P. "Let's go!"

"All aboard!" the conductor called.

T. P. and Bluebonnet jumped off the caboose and ran across the depot yard.

T. P. reached the train first and hopped up on the step of a passenger car. "C'mon, Bluebonnet," he shouted. Bluebonnet was running as fast as she could.

Whoooo! Whoooooo!

"Hurry, Bluebonnet!" T. P. called. "The train is about to leave!"

With his claws outstretched, T. P. reached down and caught Bluebonnet by her sunbonnet and pulled her aboard. The train lurched forward as the wheels began to roll.

"Whew!" sighed Bluebonnet. "We made it!"

The cat and the armadillo found a seat by a window. "Now this," said Bluebonnet, "is a wonderful way to see the sights."

"I can't believe it!" T. P. purred happily. "I'm finally riding a train, thanks to you, Bluebonnet."

"Looks like we have a whole new adventure ahead of us," said Bluebonnet.

"And when we return," said T. P., " we'll come home . . . to the Marshall Train Depot."